To the Left of the Worshiper

T0161306

To the Left of the Worshiper

Poems by JEFFREY GREENE

alicejamesbooks

Cambridge, Massachusetts

Copyright © 1991 by Jeffrey Greene. All rights reserved.
Library of Congress Cataloging-in-Publication Data
Greene, Jeffrey
To the Left of the Worshiper.
I. Title
PS3557.R382T6   1991   811'.54—dc20   91-17407
ISBN 0-914086-93-6

Book Design and Typesetting by William Lach.
Cover photograph Cathédrale d'Autun, "Sommeil des Mages" —Chapiteau
(XIIe siecle), is reprinted by permission of Photo Editions Combier Mâcon.
Epigraph © 1978 by Oberlin College, Field Translation Series, from Eugenio
Montale's *The Storm & Other Poems* translated by Charles Wright.

*Alice James Books gratefully acknowledges support from the National Endowment for the
Arts and from the Massachusetts Council on the Arts and Humanities, a state agency whose
funds are recommended by the Governor and appropriated by the State Legislature.*

Alice James Books are published by the Alice James Poetry Cooperative, Inc.
Alice James Books, 33 Richdale Avenue, Cambridge, Massachusetts, 02140.

FOR MARY

AND IN MEMORY OF C.B.

CONTENTS

One day here two sisters came to play, two
   white butterflies, in the early hours of the
   afternoon. Toward the east the view was
   (and still is) open—and the damp rocks
   of the Corone still ripen the strong grapes
   for the 'sciacchetra.' It is curious to think
   that each of us has a country like this one,
   even if altogether different, which must
   always remain *his* landscape, unchanging;
   it is curious that the physical order of
   things is so slow to filter down into us,
   and then so impossible to drain back out.

Where the Tennis Court was . . .
                              —Montale

I. *North Star*

NIGHT DIVE

The seabeds are nocturnal.
Even on the searocks in the shallows
green crabs cling in starlight.

Boys pull on their neoprene suits
and arrive in the black ocean
looking down for lobsters.

The sealife slows under their lanterns.
In the same way the moon
would jacklight us on the bare shore.

In your right hand you can hold a lantern,
and with your left hand
you can touch the blind fish.

This is the element you love so well,
your body without light
in the ocean without light.

Tonight, Mother, I could lose you
as you sleep under the clear surface
of an oxygen tent.

I have come back to New England,
to this house where now there is no one.
I turn on lights and the rooms go on sleeping.

This is the night dive
where the slow halibut lifts like a table,
where the eel swims from a bed of skins,

and where the lobster
goes forward with its one crushing claw
and its one tearing claw.

THE ANATOMY OF NIGHT

Night comes before dark,
dark on the horizon,
night in our swimsuits and towels
where they hang on a bush,
night over the cottages
that grow whiter before they darken,
the yellow of their kitchens,
night over Cross Mills Library
lit blue with its Starlight movie,
night over the white church
and its one-room school
and Rathbone's fishhouse
with its dark crowded tanks,
night over Fort Ninigret,
two massive maples at its heart
and one boulder for thanks
to the Niantic and Narragansett Indians,
night over the bluffs where King George's
man-o'-war and two of his fireships
slipped toward New London,
night in the statuary
where one stone reads,
I would not want to live always,
the body of night in our hands,
the dreams we wake from a little sad.

THE BIRDWATCHER

I couldn't begin to tell
my stepfather what he has missed.
That would take every minute of my time.

What he has missed has nothing
to do with what has become of us.
That is of no consequence now.

In the pose of the bittern
there's a balance of forces.
It points its bill straight up
into the face of gravity.
One eye looks toward the wetlands.
One eye is planted on me.
It's as if presence
is the work of a simple brain,
a double exposure.

My stepfather believed
that we might describe the bittern,
distinguish it, making words
a part of seeing,
and, of course, they are
when balanced with affection.

How else could we talk
about the world to ourselves?
What else could sadden us more
than to be severed from the affections
of our own voices?

I can still see him
at dawn on the deck of the cottage,
the birdwatcher. The whole man I mean.

SAIL LOFT

This village is full of dry rot,
broken barrels, and cannon
stuffed with trash
aimed at the Mystic River.
Hardly anyone is here
in the midwinter wind.
Under the gallery of windows
we want to see someone
stitching sails together
for men away in schooners
or dredging on the river in oyster boats—
something human among
the bolts of cotton,
the beeswax, tar, and grommets—
women sewing eyelets.
If we could see them,
it would be worth standing here
with our hands to our faces
looking past ourselves
in museum glass, while souls
are stitched on air like friends
we promised to remember.
We crave moist handprints
on the other side of ours
as if touch, openhearted,
could carry into the future.
A nothingness of light
still falls on fabrics,
and an array of needles blacken
into thin moons for the dead
to roll between their fingers.

THE CONVERTED METHODIST CHURCH

A red balloon ball
was thrown at the knees

of children who stood
inside a ring of children.

This was a joyful execution
as was October to the trees.

All the freethinking of leaves
was brought to the earth.

On the ground the leaves
would skirt us in the gone field

behind the makeshift school,
a converted Methodist church.

The blown Queen Anne's lace
still stood in the blue-white field,

each stalk touched by radiation.
We wore new clothes

and talked to schoolmates
though I don't remember

who they were and nothing now
replaces their child bodies.

At school we voted like our parents
in mock elections or learned

how a thin membrane forms
between the tip

of a numb branch and a leaf.
The leaf flew off

like an island
shaken by revolution.

Our school orchestra
burdened with clarinets

limbered with loose
breath, bows, and keys

until one girl stood
with a broken violin.

Sympathy was the same note
hit a thousand times.

A child's father brought in
a calf's head, carefully cut

to be seen in its parts.
We traced the major vessels

that were once strung between the heart
and the palm-sized brain.

Waste keeps dividing
and gathering weight

until we grow
large enough as adults

to internalize the world.
Now windows are shut.

Leaves stir out in the light
like the distance gained

from the pain of others or friends
or a whole neighborhood

struggling in poverty.
Around are the things of adults—

the book and the diaphragm on the table,
a skirt on a heavy wooden chair.

FROM SAN FRANCISCO

The last time the world
seemed to hit something
or someone upstairs in the blue
slammed a door left ajar,
some of us were paying attention,
and some of us weren't,
and we went around asking
who felt what or saw
the glass bend toward them
or wondered if the quake
would stop or start up again.
I imagine how years from now,
praying that it will be years,
maybe beside some statuary
in a garden we will feel
a little nudge of our lives ending
and whisper to each other,
"Did you feel anything?"

In this city the weather's redundant,
each day perfect for months.
And at night the moon gazes
on the nasturtiums and Japanese tile.
One night it gazed on me
when I couldn't sleep
with a cracked tooth.
Early that morning,
we drove through the city
looking for painkillers
while the wind blew
and numberless traffic signals
changed for no one
against the powdered sky.

The other night at dinner
the talk was about death rituals—
the need to see the dead in person
so they don't come back
living in our dreams.
I remembered how the Anglo-Saxons
sometimes buried the head
apart from the body
to keep the dead from wandering back whole
and shaking the thatch.
In *The Gazette of Old English Burial Sites*,
they listed one skull full of nuts
collected there by a squirrel
the way some of us keep track
of our worst years.

My stepfather, whom I never saw buried,
had his small service in springtime
in Southington, Connecticut.
My mother called, and we talked awhile
when the world seemed to hit something
and no one else felt it.

NORTH STAR

Wilton, Connecticut

I.

One wish will be granted—
you will be invisible,
you will vanish from the ring of children
whose names vanish but for the few
whom you will still wonder about.
They turn on the circle painted on asphalt.

            And you will walk out
of the schoolyard past the leaves
blown under the cold monkey bars,
the pile of dead summer scrolls.

            You will regret
that you missed the story hour,
that you missed the ending of something
before beginning again
as you learn to leave off what you cannot finish,
that fragments like river ice
shift hard on each other.

You touch what a child dreams about—
that which flies, floats, or moves the earth
and makes a hobby of assembling pieces.

Or you go down to the community swimming pond
where you held your breath so long
that a few on shore shifted nervously.

You can walk to the place where you broke the surface
held in the black impenetrable ice like the stiff reed and leaf,
where the sun goes down red flaming without heat,
in the place you came from.

II.

The snow is one surface replacing another,
erasing the variances in the plain hour of the day,
in the tree that crowds the window
and nests the snow, the snow that sees
into the silent heart of the woods.
Nothing between the hand and the fire,
the voice and the hour, the mouth and the tear.
Your lover opens to your touch,
and you are already enfolded, cradled,
her mouth over your ear
urging you to go now, go now,
with all the force of your eagerness
as into a childhood meadow.
Once your mother wept
for a man who was not your father.
In your heaviness you stood like a tree
since sadness must have a body.
The more you tried to think of nothing,
the more your body gathered meaning,
the branches lowered as they are lowered at the window,
the arms that accumulate sympathy
and the naked darkness
of your lover kneeling over you, opening the small of her back
and arching herself gently down on you,
one surface replacing another
where you and the child in you are buried.

III.

Buried in the ovate leaves of the lilac
are the secrets of the homestead and the hidden traveler
conversant with the North Star
alone in its magnitude in the woods.

From the secret stairway under the slopes
of the gambrel roof, down to the cellar
and the roots of the weeping willow,
you can trace the Underground Railway.

You thought that slaves rode a sort of invisible subway
below the muffled dogs and search parties,
below the sultry southern trees
flashing with torches you'd seen in movies.
But the engine passes in the ground,

its whistle blowing so far north
it freezes mid-air under the guiding star,
where the magnetized pin points dancing on a thread,
where your father points, blue polestar,
where you mumbled the same words before daydreaming
    classmates
that Lincoln spoke before utter ruin,
and where the avenging angel disintegrates
into the blue-white flakes.

II. *To the Left of the Worshiper*

TO THE LEFT OF THE WORSHIPER

North, n. [ME.; AS.; akin to D. noord, *G.* nord; *IE.*
base *ner-, *beneath, below: said to be so called from*
being left of the worshipers praying to the East]
—Webster's New World Dictionary

Leaving on my birthday, I joked a rebirth
from the towers downtown that loomed
glass giants reimagining the sky
above the dwarfed settlement house
at Allen's Landing on the bayou's shallow gulch—
pink, silver, black geometrical sky
far over the mists of Hermann Park,
the sleeping zoo, and Sam Houston
pointing from his traffic circle
to the fiery east, where from the towers
you can see the refineries blow
burn-off fire. Under the art museum banners
the shadows are filled with the dew-wet
bronze nudes. I passed them going north
to the commercial district's commingling
democracy of billboards, Mexican bars,
and car lots. Single story shacks
link the whole inner circle of the city
inside the beltway circle of gunfire,
domestic squabbles, and the wanderers
who shower with their sacks of aluminum cans
under sprinklers on bank lawns
in late May. I loved you
and stopped to phone as the wind
picked up and blew around the booth
and jets roared toward Houston International.
I had not slept since we stood on
Shakespeare Street at 1 a.m.,
the whole neighborhood under
the southern light of the Astrodome,
dousing the fire of the stars,

blackening the water oak and its pigmy leaves
where one night my neighbor sat
and howled like an animal
even with the red and white lights
of the powder-blue patrol car
flicking circles below. Nothing sleeps,
only the flesh chills down
in the numbed dark, the tired pumps
of air-conditioners, the condensation watering
the stargrass and morning glories.
Nobody sleeps. Not the programmer
upstairs with her blond Izod clean-cut
mounting her, nor the full-grown man with his
misshapen human utterances home again
with his mother. They are bonded to some curse
that exceeds reasonable human suffering.
Yet that night the city became gentle
as the nighthawks chirped and swooped.
I tried to call you from Queen City
before Texarkana, where the wind blows
dizzy with dust or pollen among
people of another world than
the one we parted in, the two of us
in the parking lot under the nighthawks,
counting the mysteries of what love
we welcomed, intruded upon, or could not prevent—
the body, the fire and roses, filled
with ingenious desires for the improbable.
And I called you from outside
of Memphis, and then Louisville,
and then gave up, passing upper Ohio
into Pennsylvania. Another night had passed,
when a fire was started, a fire accompanied
by such damage as to leave nothing,
a fire that caught the grasses,
the tops of trees, the highway

rising to the Alleghenies, raging bright,
bright yellow as the mornings
when I woke, a child in the north,
the sun to the east, and learned to worship.

THE SUBTENDER

Banks of fog
would wait in force
until the heat faltered
in the California valleys.
Then they'd come
and beach themselves
on the coastal hills.
Erasure starts with the limbs
and the leaves of the scrub oaks,
with the seas of the daytime moon.
This is how the shades
of afternoon moved into evening
at Año Nuevo. Strollers gathered
at one end of the beach
where the well-intentioned
conservationist shot a sea lion
with darts of anesthesia.
In spite of her illness
and the drug, she willed her way
against the traffic of waves.
When she slept
and when she washed back,
something of sweetness
remained in her face.
The gulls came to feed on her.

On another coast I am looking
at an old subtender,
its gray hull rising above me
from the black water of the channel,
the waves flexing with light.
The hum of generators
deep inside must also run
through the bodies of 18-year-olds
who enlisted from all parts

of the country. Some are reading
in the bare light.
Some are filtering
into the city on leave.
Each of us has a place
that is singular in memory
like the subtender at sea.
Black submarines maneuver,
waiting to attach themselves
to the huge curvature of the hull.

LOUISIANA

Traffic halts for a wreck
on the causeway, while we
are delirious with travel
before sunrise. We look out
at the swamp, starless now,
still water on both sides,
cypresses dressed in mosses
that make them weep.
We feel sorry for whoever
they are in crushed cars
and spreading fluids, knowing
our own terror lies before us,
not in what kills us
but in how we are severed
from our loves. Maybe
the dead linger by their bodies,
witnesses, as are the tall
white waterfowl in the trees.
Last night we sang to stay awake,
believing the will
is stronger than sleep,
while the cities we passed
were corrosive to the heart,
the bridges and refineries
strung with lights and fires.
One was more like hell
than the last. The cars
have yet to loosen,
the living look ahead
while a hunter's boat
speeds into the bright bayou.

THE COAT

Nobody wears the coat
that holds the form of the body

with sweat and carbon from passing diesels.
Left on the switching bar,

it looks like someone standing there,
zipped to the collar, thankful for what

nobody could put a finger on—
the morning comes to it on rails.

It's up to everyone else to pursue happiness
now after spring, and be thankful

for the coolness keeping down mosquitoes
that breed in the sauce can or the palm

of a rubber glove. Propane
whispers to the kitchens near the tracks,

and one trash can stands as the left
foul line for the softball diamond

of chipped tile, cinders, and dirt.
This lot is still wet from the night,

quiet between fellowships of mourning doves,
the unemployed, and neighborhood athletes,

tall and mythical. The myth of the coat
is idleness, someone meditating

day after day, whispering about joy
under the blue sky. The same blue

pours through the charred roof
of the church and holds together

all the fragments of the city. Everything
is clear around the glittering tracks,

the shotgun houses with holes in their screens
for faces, cats, or fans whirring

through the sounds of pleasure, yielding
to exhaustion in the room's dark. Nothing

can be done with troubles, and tasks aren't
a matter of courage, since idleness has no hands.

THE LIE

LIFE IN THE PAST

Bring it back to life, love,
   not out of the truth
which is both too little
   and too much for us
but out of the dream
   that we added to truth
to make it bearable.
   Whole years
are nothing now,
   far off and distant,
sleeping in our senses.
   Therefore this light
without you is both
   agony and relief.
But I will wait for you,
   maybe all day by agreement,
by the pond in the city.
   I have nowhere in particular
that I must go,
   so I watch the children
in a train scaled down
   to carry them under
the park pines and past
   the white obelisk
and Sam Houston
   on his bronze horse
pointing to the salt flats
   of San Jacinto.
The children return in joy
   as they started.
If you come, bring the boys—
   Abram with his thick
black hair and Emilio

with a smile that haunts
of his father.
    They will not remember me
when they sleep finally
    in the fullness of their day.
I will hold you so that
    these odors and shadows
will bring you back
    almost physically.

THE SEPARATION

She pours out a pool of red paint
    and with a white paper straw
between her lips she blows
    the shapes of trees.

When her two boys blow too
    at what she starts, they will form
a red forest. I am trying to picture this
    from what she has told me.

Now she has returned to otherness,
    and when she calls she will say
she was up more than once
    rubbing Abram's small legs

that ache from playing too hard.
    The moon is unearthed
over Avenue C. It rises
    over her father's white truck

and over the old elementary school
    with white paper faces.
It rises over the church with a hole
    burnt through the roof

and the Mother of God, who did not move
    from mildness where she stood
in flames that grew like a forest.
    It's hard to crave so much

as if the flames were blown into us.
    This is the moon in spring
in the city. It should be a parting
    from recklessness into sleep.

Now in her thirties,
    two children, she reads Melville,
who says two-thirds
    of a man is darkness
like the oceans of the world.
    She puts down the book
and recalls how the boys
    were dressed
for the church festival,
    a devil and a drunk.

They did not win
    for their costumes
but performed ad-lib
    for friends and made
their own festival
    carrying colored paper sacks.
Sometimes she sees
    the men in them.
What Melville names
    means little to her,

but in the absence of love
    she could see an ocean,
vast, incomprehensible.
    She remembers Mexico City,
the vendors and napkins,
    thousands of them
with the image of the Virgin
    among the crowds and dust
at the Basilica.
    This was her honeymoon,

years ago. The hotel in the evening
    was light blue,
the air was close, human.
    She dreamed passion
would come like a vision
    with the partial moon,
the trumpet and the roses in the arbor
    where the dogs barked.
She thought her husband
    would magnify like the roses.

THE LOVE OF DAUGHTERS

She tells me I have arms
    like Julio's.
This is not the first time
    she has said that.
What are a father's arms
    to his daughter—
the good in men? Their gentleness?
    Julio is out of work
and sullen. The kids
    avoid him and battle
in their rooms. Maybe
    he could make things
out of wood and sell them
    at the flea market
down the Avenue, but nothing
    sounds right. How could it?
It is so hot and sticky
    that even dogs
creep into the bars
    for shade. Insects
deafen the trees
    and the world divides
into nostalgia and indifference.
    There must be hours
when Julio imagines
    himself dead, and perceptions
come to him
    one by one like phantoms,
the old wooden stools and beer,
    phantoms from the night before,
and before that,
    the huge past, the dark walks

and houses at 2 a.m.,
    a room with a woman
not so long ago,
    a particular odor,
a particular grief
    like a city. He knows
his daughter has seen her.
    Her forgiveness
is immeasurable as the past,
    or she has simply learned
to live without her father.
    Sometimes we imagine
a child together.
    She calls her Rosina and laughs
saying, "You know you can have her,"
    undoing the button
to her jeans, "but you
    don't want her."

THE AWAKENING

Wake up, Julio,
    wake to a child's thing
that shines of thin metal
    and goes around
powered by a spring.
    It's not over yet,
the monotonous rail freight
    that passes through the neighborhood,
the night thick
    with chemical odors
and the ringing
    of the red-eyed crossing gate.
Your wife is older,
    but look how she touches you
as if you were a child blessed.
    You could remember
listening as a child
    to the nighthawks chirp
as they collect mosquitoes
    over the lettered avenues.
But this is winter,
    and you are dreaming
of someone gone for a long time,
    someone you almost remember.
It is your father
    or your father-in-law
in this shadowed room
    or one of your brothers
at the coffee factory,
    his mind like a knife,
imagining the endless
    charity of women.
You have outlived them all

leaving them in some impossible world,
a pure white ball.
    Wake now to the calendar
with golden angels
    and the Virgin in December
among the farm animals.
    Gina and Theresa are grown.
They argue with their husbands
    and come around in tears.
Abram and Emilio
    go through your pockets
knowing that you left
    coins for them.
Wake up, Julio,
    to a child's toy
that comes around,
    geared down, tapping
at your shoe.
    You are not an immovable
fragment of moon
    like your Spanish father,
nor are you stuck
    in a chair at the hospital
waiting for someone
    to be born or to die.
You are not holding flowers
    as you did in other times
in another life
    when you still
had to sweat it out.

[43]

THE SUNKEN CATHEDRAL

She worries about Abram's
   troubles in a white kids' school
and rages inside against his teacher
   who also worries, like an insult.
It is almost too quiet.
   A plate stands on the bureau,
a moon, a rose
   glazed into it,
and an oval frame contains
   a god she hardly
remembers to think about.
   What should she say to Abram?
That she loved school herself?
   That she loved to watch
for the bus as it
   arrived down Avenue C
she thought to save her?
   And what should she say about school?
About love and encouragement?
   How she studied
in the empty music room
   Debussy's "The Sunken Cathedral"
on a cheap cassette,
   and the cathedral would rise
out of the waters of the lost
   (those afternoons), the bells
and then the vespers.
   She loved Bartok's
"4th String Quartet"
   because she understood it,
the night sounds.
   What is discipline if not
the love of approval

or devotion in poverty,
hours of practicing
    her instrument in a closet
against the muted acoustics
    of her mother's dresses?
She watches Abram run
    in the small fenced yard
and knows how children
    love to run. She remembers
running herself, mindlessly
    over hard ground.

THE LIE

Under the ancient ahuehuete
   in Mexico City, Cortes wept
over his disastrous defeat.
   This was before he
utterly destroyed the Aztecs.
   The tree is now shaped
as if it grew out of anger,
   twisted and branching
into subtler passions
   and suffering. What is it

rooted to under the city?
   Another time, the same city
founded on a myth of roses
   and the Virgin opening
a robe of stars, the moon
   supported under her feet
by angels encircling
   the hills and muddy water.
She is a symbol of the conservatives,
   painted purple, white, and gold

and nailed in place
   by a 16th-century carpenter.
In Houston, they let
   the crazies out
in the middle of the city,
   and they drift

into the neighborhoods, weeping
    sometimes in the streets
as darkly as Cortes,
    destruction on destruction.

Gina got up from bed
    and went to one
to chase some horror
    out of him. She must have
appeared as the guardian
    of his heart, her soft
face, her encouragement.
    Who knows what feats
he went on to accomplish
    in the dazing heat

and local trash
    or how he was brought down
finally? Gina says
    she never weeps
unless she is angry,
    which is not the truth.
I remember on the phone once
    out of loneliness she wept
a huge immovable silence
    that still roots in me.

III. *A Portrait for Mary*

THE BELLS AT SAINT-AIGNAN

for Jacques and Lena

The bells at the Romanesque church of Saint-Aignan
were christened after the names of certain noble women.
They were also named after bees and wasps as well as
after the notes they sounded. So each bell has three names.

These women live aloft
while their namesakes have walked the earth,
loved, and long ago
discarded in pain

their human bones. Their voices
come down the tiers in the blue air,
peal major second, third, and fifth
down to the roses,

down to the banks of the slow Cher
whose shallow green
records the town in complete silence
of the sunken world. Marie

counts the hours,
little Françoise the quarter hours,
as from their shoulders they swing
in their bronze dresses.

Hélène, Magdelaine, Emma
ring for the mass
or a saint's day, if you look below
to watch the people

decorate their town and dance in a tent
under the swallows. Someone
who sweeps a bee from her dress
hears the resonance

on earth as in the tower,
an E major,
while the wasp is in D and the bourdon is in C.
So the bells, the wasps, and the women

form a complicity
of place in summer: the women in the public gardens,
the wasps in the eaves,
the bells for the newly married and the dead

and the faith they keep in time
having known all
of the town ghosts in their weather-beaten corner
and those who pass below

that windy space
of bells and nesting birds
where bellringers have been blown from the earth
in summer storms.

The women would stand like stone in the air
until the next bellringer
rang them the next day and the day after
when children talk

to their invisible friends
as they walk with nothing to do
in their own short time
along the wall or down the lane.

THE OCTOPUS

Something that blushes
    open-eyed and comical
touches in us a place
    of sympathy or sadness
since it has a human
    weakness of its own,
feeling in each direction
    across hard or slippery surfaces
until it finds a closed-in place
    it can't resist
and makes a home.
    Of course, the fishermen
know this, dropping by rope
    terra cotta pots.
The octopus loves
    what it finds inside
the perfectly smooth lip
    into which it slips
a tentacle to circle
    the black space,
discovering no corners,
    and then arm by arm
enters wholly
    only to be drawn up
into the blue light of heaven.

THE HORSES OF AUTUMN

I cannot stop here long,
   only long enough to watch
the guard crossing
   Pont de la Tournelle on horseback.
They ride in twos through the mist
   and disappear into the poplars,
yellow now, giving up their leaves steadily.
   The time has changed,
but not all at once.
   It felt something far off and cold
and does not linger.
   I must move on,
but remain under this spell:
   no more beautiful cities
could make you well.
   I wish we could sit
in the warm air by the tall windows,
   up where impatiens bloom
red and white in the boxes.
   You could come back
as one who has not slept,
   as one who walks long before Paris
awakens, the shops entombed
   behind their shutters, the towers
alone in the light, and the streets
   where Napoleon strolled
in his morning disguises
   plotting works to modernize
an aging world. If you come

I'd rather you bring your grievances
against the poverty of the invisible
   than to have the awful
dreams and half-exhausted nights
   of adjusting. But no rhetoric works
between you and the living
   because there is no common ground,
no likenesses needed
   even to wage a losing war.

ON AUGUSTA

The cottage at night, the roses,
the local songs the four girls
from Oberhasli sang are all
Byron wrote from Switzerland
to his half-sister. Today the wind
comes and blows south to north
bringing mild headaches and making
cows complain up in the crags.
Foam gathers like lake ghosts,
the wind giving them no peace
against the walls of Chillon,
where we go to see Byron's name
scratched into one pillar
in the dungeon, his holy place.
Suffering has been put to rest there.
What we love about the wind,
the lake, and the sad castle
comes to us in two voices.
One is always our own, what we
describe to ourselves, and the other,
if we are lucky, is right beside us.
For Byron it was Augusta.
What she might love he described
setting out again with servants,
carriages, and saddlehorses
for the mountains and glaciers
he called frozen hurricanes.

A PORTRAIT FOR MARY

I.

I checked out of the small American Library
Williams reading in 1958.
I thought you'd like to hear him—
the poems, though personal,
are not so difficult to take in.
"The Descent," "The Orchestra," "To Elsie."
He says in "To Daphne and Virginia"
that he loves all women but touches them
confused like other men. He hesitates,
losing the thought, as if he doesn't
recognize what he has written
or stumbles through the rhythm of something new.
In the background on the recording,
there are the sounds of traffic, horns,
a kind of poetic theory, things themselves
purifying language. They are also the sounds
of things from my childhood,
so they come back, making a plain argument
with the present. They come back
also in talk, to go over again one's life
when love is new and grows older,
a process of remembering for someone else
by way of introductions
and the heart's interests not unlike a poem.
So the sounds of traffic bring to mind
the vague shapes of cars, Bel Air, Fairlane.
Some sat in the yard so long
that the landscape seemed barren without them,
sinking to their rims, until by chain
they were towed out of our lives.
Saturdays went up in smoke.
I could show you a photograph
in which the house is lost in a snowdrift,
four rooms, a pure white tunnel

to the door, my father's Dixieland
permeating our burial. February and still the gold
Christmas decorations hung from the beam.
Impressions come back, the sky and the earth,
one milky consistency, Sundays in January,
the frozen pond, the dark brown horses
harnessed to a sled, the sled rising
on the hill, nothing dead but sleeping,
nothing permanent but passing, passing away.
When I turn on my back, having lifted myself
from your body, now at rest beside me,
we talk for hours. I can
toss off the present like a sheet
and remember the horses. I could describe
the bridge in summer, where we set up
a telescope in the dark to see the pure
sphere of Saturn inside a hard ring of gasses,
the storm of Jupiter, and Echo,
the silver speck racing over a field of stars.
I came back there to walk,
the trash dumped under the raspberry branches,
the waterfall, a rushing white spirit,
a soaked pornographic magazine
that teenagers had left open to a Latin woman,
her buttocks turned toward the camera.
It seemed as incongruous as the nights
my mother wore a blue costume,
nothing to it, and worked a second job
late at the Midtown Motor Inn,
the most difficult time of her life.
My father lived in a storefront in Queens,
and my brother and I listened to the same record
spinning endlessly before us—
"An angel watches over my love."

In the photographs from childhood,
I could show you there is nothing
sad about my parents, nothing about the quiet
negotiations toward separation,
unspoken changes of heart. We must
be sorry for the way photographs
are false witnesses to love.
It is better that they are acts
of imagination, as Williams says in "Asphodel,"
to watch the flight of time.
It is better if I describe
what goes unfinished and comes back—
divorce, mysteries, ramifications.
It was too easy to drop out of high school,
too easy to leave the stiff
formalin worm and the scalpel,
the guys getting blown in the john,
fifty laps in heavy chlorination,
and the debate in which I was,
of all people, Rutherford B. Hayes.
It was almost too easy,
so the same things go unfinished,
and I go back in dreams in my adult body
to the corridors, to the Latin teacher,
Puella parva Romana est.
In truth it ends with a train at night,
the tired lights of the stations,
and then the bath after days of no sleep in jail,
but what I remember most
is the fear of sleep, that I might
awake to the gray enamel again,
like a ship, below decks, the same

AWOL addict agonizing in the next cell
until they silenced him, putting him
somewhere out of reach.
I had a Styrofoam cup on which I had scratched,
having seen my father's face
afloat behind the wire mesh screen,
a message to myself. Just writing
was an act against dreaming.

II.

Troubles that seemed so great once
appear smaller, and half-smiling, we have
a few tricks to get us through
some anxious times, as my mother carries
in her purse a photograph of a particular
beach that she loves, that calms her,
a place not so beautiful that it distances,
but one that embraces, its small road
down to the shore, the white cottages here and there,
the potato fields down to the ocean.
Some photographs we must be sorry for,
events set in motion that must be
allowed to fulfill themselves,
the war in Vietnam completing itself
in photographs. For some of us
only one night was a gamble in the draft.
We listened to the lottery, birth date and number,
birth date and number, over the radio.
Some of us simply won out.
Living in the Midwest, I loved
to visit Lesley in her studio,
the turpentine, the odor of pines,
the models she worked from. Everything counted,

the color pack and the shadows, the looping
cut-out paper, the resistance to words.
I loved the towering windows of
the Old Music Building, to walk there
in the dark. Some nights the stars hung
above the dome of the Capitol,
some winters the wind blew 30 m.p.h.
at 15 below, the wind rounding the corner
at the Savings and Loan, rounding the
frozen Woolworth's in an uninhabitable world
(except beside the ringing radiators
in Lesley's studio). New love grows older,
as if two have cared for a third,
a combination of selves, perspectives
bound up in each other. Something has already
started in you and me almost imperceptibly,
a history recording itself. It is almost
impossible to remember how it begins
though it roots between the self and no self.
One spring, Lesley and I cared for my grandmother.
She worked in the garden, holding a trowel
over the yellow heads of marigolds,
the green tubes connected to a portable supply
of oxygen. We were ghosts she
almost recognized in the world of the living.
Muhammad Ali was fighting late in his career
on the TV screen beside her bed,
and she simply stopped breathing.
In "The Last Words of My English Grandmother,"
Williams' grandmother rode in from West Haven.
Mine, wrapped in a black blanket,
rode down Whitney Avenue.
New cities unravel as if you pull
a thread from a bobbin, and you can follow
the thread back to an unfamiliar place,
so that there are two cities:

the first one is always unknown,
and the second is the one you live in.
Nights in California, we could see
Twin Peaks from our bed, and think of the Jeffers poem—
the city caught in a net, the lights
flickering as if fighting to free themselves.
We struggle to believe the worst news—
you remember—the phone call
about my cousin C.B.'s death. Grief also unravels
so I can follow it back
to drinking beer after work with C.B.,
my own age. Or follow it back to childhood
and the country without knowing
what kind of men we'd become.
Out from the crescent shore of Half Moon Bay,
C.B.'s ashes were tossed in the Pacific—
how easily they sift through the nets now.
Lesley and I drove along the Rhone in a red Volvo,
across the Pyrenees and the vast
plateaus of Spain, the sorrowful rock hovels.
Madrid, Toledo, and down to Granada,
where Williams also stood at the Alhambra
getting directions from the Gypsy women.
He must have seen the swallows,
how they dip and rise through the seam
of shadows on the high wall
and through the star dome over the bath
for the Moorish concubines, the swallows
racing through the cut-out stars.
Then to Portugal, the vineyards, the almond trees,
the boats on the horizon with lanterns.
What goes unfinished comes back,
the last time I saw Lesley in the cool
swept rooms of the farmhouse where moths
were trapped when we first arrived.

How did they get there? Did they
crawl through in another shape
only to transform? They exited then
in the night air, given the chance.

III.

In a garage apartment behind a strip shack in Texas,
I swear that when you lie on your stomach,
a pistol to your head, you can have
two thoughts at once: that you are alive
and you wish that you had drugs
or money to bargain with. And after,
you feel you have come up for air,
the night, the water oaks under the hot stars—
everything is new and tired also.
I remember the year that one of my students
was sick so that I could see for months
there was no suspense in his body:
how could he profit from the lectures I gave him
on agents of plot, the intervention
of gods to elevate events?
A call from the hospice, and I
thought of him, his weighty anthology,
Aeneas in the underworld and cold Dido.
You can look in the city pond,
a flash through the murk, the carp, bronze
as I imagine the shields of the Greeks,
Aeneas' agonizing search for Creusa.
But there I remember the Vietnamese fishing
from the muddy shore, only a few years back,
it seems, before the banks were set
in concrete. Now friends stay behind,
and each lover stands in impossible bounds
like Creusa, neither life nor death,

neither ending nor beginning again.
Remember this fall in Paris, there were evenings
that changed us, the destruction,
the terrorist blasts, and yet
no one stopped to wonder. People
gazed at churches or walked home.
The ambulances, one after another,
arrived and went with their writhing cargo.
Then again, another blast and the commerçants
stood dumbfounded in front of their businesses.
Shoppers just fell randomly among the racks
of clothes on Rennes. The ambulances
came unrelenting, each one lowering
our hearts by increments. Yet in the morning
I wake by increments, when you are still sleeping,
the birds at song echoing in the courtyard,
the concierge firing a hard stream
from the hose into the bottom of a trash can.
I can remember the exact sounds of birds
from the country, growing up, the echo
in the trees and down over the small stream.
The day begins also with remembered things
or, as Breton said, with beauty confounded
by innocence. Sometimes I would
try to imagine someone right now, say,
watering plants, airing out a room somewhere,
who will know me as no one else knows me.
We embark through the layers of days, reading
The Tribune, walking out to Luxembourg Gardens,
watching the tennis players work toward
some invincible image of themselves.
Or we stand in front of the Medici fountain
under the chestnut trees, the pool,
the embrace of Galetea and Acis
just before the jealous Cyclops

crushes Acis, turning him into a river.
Spring 1987, we are listening to Williams read
"To Daphne and Virginia" on a cassette.
Two cats sleep on the heater, three roses
on tall stems. My friends Michael and Bridget
have a son, Gareth. Do you ever think
of how names change, a coordinating conjunction,
my friends Gary and Connie, their children
Jackie and Timothy, or Scott and Jane
and Alexander and Laura? We listen to Williams,
the unsteady cadence of his voice
and the thick sounds of traffic.

ARRIVALS

Waiting for you at Arrivals,
Kennedy Airport, your flight delayed
for hours, it seems as if you are hoping
for the right words, said or thought,
to coax you down. I remember
a different world than this
expectant crowd gathered
at the corridor to customs.
I remember a town full of towers.
We had rented a room next to
the Sacristy and the Cloisters
of Mercy and the marble stones
of the public cemetery. Our one window
under the eaves looked out
on the skewed aerials of San Gimignano
and the workshop of Mr. Marrucci,
our landlord. He taped
a collection of photographs to the door—
"The Tuba Player" by Robert Frank,
The World Trade Center in Manhattan,
and one of himself
making a coffin. The old men gathered
on the stone bench, not a woman
among them, nor was Marrucci
whom we saw each night in a chair
beside the window, listening to his wife
and her friend below and watching
the girls at games on the steps
of St. Agostino. At five in the heat,
you closed the shutters
and took off your clothes.
We made love quietly, fearing we'd
be overheard, though it was unnecessary
given the racket from boys
racing their Piaggios and Moto Guzzis
between the hospital of Santa Fina

and the fortress. I took a black and white
photograph of you sitting up
in bed, the white sheet
wrapped across your breasts.
Somehow I caught a portrait of Christ
the Marruccis had hung. His hand
is extended, offering his own
gashed heart. Earlier we had seen
the frescoes by Bartolo di Fredi
and Benozzo Gozzoli, Sebastian littered
with arrows, each half a shaft deep,
and the Devil slaughtering the soldiers
and the herds of Job. There was also
the Chapel of Santa Fina, the little girl
who bore in serene resignation
Gregory's announcement of her death.
The town was compensated for the girl
with simple miracles, the bells
and spontaneous flowers. Then we climbed
the Ghibelline tower, and while coming
back down you felt yourself falling.
Was it a lack of faith? Paralysis?
I held you there, held you up,
no small effort to let you go
step by step into happiness again.

NOTES

Some phrases in "Life in the Past" are adapted from anonymous commentary that appeared in "Dope, The New Vice: Part V. The Woe of Women," *Everyday Life*, 5 November 1909.

I am indebted to Susan Sontag's *On Photography*, which informs some of the ideas in "A Portrait for Mary."

Special thanks to Susan Prospere and Marty McGovern for their wisdom on these poems and also to Tom Cobb and Charles Siebert for their comaraderie and support.

ACKNOWLEDGMENTS

Grateful acknowledgment is made to the following publications in which the listed poems have appeared:

The American Scholar: "The Subtender."

The Antioch Review: "On Augusta."

Crazyhorse: "The Lie," "The Sunken Cathedral."

The Denver Quarterly: "A Portrait for Mary."

Domestic Crude: "From San Francisco."

High Plains Literary Review: "The Octopus."

The Indiana Review: "The Love of Daughters."

The Iowa Review: "The Birdwatcher."

The Missouri Review: "The Coat."

The Nebraska Review: "The Awakening" (published as "Portrait of Julio").

The New Yorker: "Louisiana."

Prairie Schooner: "Love of the Faithless," "The Separation."

River City: "Arrivals."

The Seattle Review: "Night Dive."

The Seneca Review: "The Horses of Autumn."

The Sewanee Review: "The Anatomy of Night," "Sail Loft."

Tendril: "The Converted Methodist Church" (published as "Makeshift").

Thanks to the Cullen Foundation, the Mary Roberts Rinehart Foundation, and the University of New Haven for support that helped make this book possible.